MW00655039

Fear:
The Basis of
Our Functioning
The Courage to See Self

By W.O. Bartle, Jr.

"Hopefully, this understanding will be of help to people and society."

W.O. Bartle, Jr.

Copyright© 2002 by W.O. Bartle, Jr.
Library of Congress Number: Copyright pending.
ISBN#: 0-9725441-0-0 Hardcover

All rights reserved. No part of this book may be reproduced or
transmitted in any form or by any means, electronic or mechanical
including photocopying, recording, or by any information storage
and retrieval system, without permission in writing from the copyright
owner.

Printed in the United States
Design and Photography by Cory Weibye.

Second Printing.

Table Of Contents

I. Introduction to Fear

Fear is the basis of our functioning in work, health and relationships – our lives. Fear is the basis of our mostly unconscious decision making and therefore our functioning. Our fear is "what is going to happen to me"? That concern dictates that our decisions be compromised. Our decisions are basically attempts at self-protection. That prejudice is defensive. Defensiveness is a response to our fear. Defensiveness is an attempt at self-protection. Defensiveness compromises objectivity, the truth and effectiveness. Defensiveness and success are not compatible. Every person is defensive in varying degrees because of their basic fear. The purpose of this understanding is to define the cause of our dominating fear. Understanding this cause can liberate us from our controlling fear, if we have the courage.

Our fear is primarily rooted in emotion and feelings. Intellect is important. However, if intellect was the answer to success, then all high IQ or educated people would be successful. That is not the case. We measure success on a comparative basis, which is defensive and self apology. That means we let others set our standard. We accept being average and conventional – normal. Average is not independent, creative or individual. It is limiting because of our fear. Emotions and feelings dominate intellect. We ask each other: "How do you feel?" We don't ask, "How do you think"? In essence, we are saying our feelings are more important and dominant than our intellect. Defensively, we use our intellect to attempt to rationalize and justify our decisions and actions. Paradoxically, we have the same brain and therefore the same intellectual capacity as Albert Einstein, but we compromise, inhibit and stifle our thinking and functioning. We are rationalizing titans to our own detriment. We lack the emotional understanding of our fear. We withdraw from and avoid our feelings. Our withdrawal from and avoidance of our feelings are attempts at self-protection from our fear. These rationalizations are attempts to satisfy our dominating need for security. Our controlling need for security is a product of our fear. Our defensive efforts for security avoid objectivity and effectiveness. We defeat ourselves and reinforce our insecurity. We attempt to allay our fear and insecurity by noting that other people do the same thing; hopefully there is safety or security in numbers. Until we recognize our fear, we will continue to compromise and defeat ourselves. We have one enemy, ourselves. What then is the basis of our fear? The basics!

Our fear is of opening, flexibility, change, separation, closeness, our own assertiveness/aggressiveness and success. Our fear is of our own exposure. Our fear is of showing and asserting ourselves and of change and success. We keep our fear deep, unconscious and buried even from ourselves. That is trying and fatiguing work. It is the opposite of relaxed. It includes those times when we have to show and assert ourselves, no matter how subtle it seems. It is when we are singled out and exposed as an individual. It is the case from the boardroom to the bedroom. That can be talking, speaking up especially about self and our feelings or giving a speech. It is pronounced in showing feelings, especially love, even to a mate. That fear and avoidance is the main obstacle to openness, closeness, joy and love/success in life and marriage. We have chosen to remain unconscious because of the power and threat of our fear. People say they want to succeed, yet they make rationalized decisions that they feel will protect them, but in doing so avoid objectivity, assertiveness and success. I think it is better to go by what people do, than by what they say. Regrettably, because of our fear of showing and asserting ourselves, we seldom hear people admitting a mistake, even to ourselves. That is dishonest. It is cheating ourselves because of our basic fear. Having to rationalize that you are perfect is naïve, defensive and an insight into our insecurity. If we cannot admit a mistake, we can't change. If we can't change, we can't improve. If we can't improve, we can't succeed. We are stuck in childhood or emotional adolescence. Our fear of opening and showing and asserting ourselves defeats us. We avoid success. We procrastinate rather than show and assert ourselves. Brilliant is admired and flattering, but effective is successful. Effectiveness requires showing and asserting ourselves. If we can't show and assert ourselves we are in neutral, not in gear. We go nowhere in life. Our fear is the basis of our functioning in work, health and relationships - our lives.

II. Work

Our fear is the primary obstacle in work. Workers are limited by their fear of showing and asserting themselves; whether blue collar or white collar. It is the primary obstacle in business. In an effort to avoid showing and asserting ourselves we have created corporations to act as an individual, but with the protection and security of the corporation. We have boards of directors and committees to avoid individual decision making and responsibility. We hide self. We choose to avoid independence and freedom, while maintaining that is what we want. Inventing the idea of a corporation is a testimonial to the creative extreme we revert to in order to not show and assert ourselves. We use the corporation for our own security. We feel the corporation will take care of us. With that fear attitude we are of minor benefit to the corporation. Instead of being taken care of by the company, we are supposed to take care of the company. The corporation takes care of managers. A leader takes care of the company. A leader aggressively drives the company to victory and success regardless of the type of business. The leader has the courage to be aggressive and produce.

Reduced fear creates a leader. We have thousands of managers, but few leaders. A leader is more secure and able to show and assert him/her self and change and succeed. A leader is independent. He can tolerate aloneness. He does not have to have the security of approval by others. For example, independent decisions and functioning is why the commodity business is frightening. You are on your own and alone, even though the potential for success is possible. In commodities or other markets, shorting is not conventional. It is frightening and seldom used. However, it is usually more decisive and faster than long, as the stock market fall of 2001 indicated. That market fall was in large part because investors and financial houses needed the security to be bulls, to have something to hold onto and unable to change. That inability to be flexible and change by liquidating their long positions cost them huge loses, instead of being short and making substantial profits. There has to be movement in order to profit in markets or life. Frozen emotionally is a product of our fear and an act against ourselves, including markets.

In our jobs we put emphasis on hard work. Hard work is noble. However, if we are working hard but with the wrong premise or understanding, we continue to defeat ourselves and avoid success. An incorrect premise insures incorrect answers and results. The correct premise allows effective results. While hard work is honorable, effective work succeeds.

It is often recommended that we own a large and diverse portfolio of stocks. The idea and goal being that if the market goes down, you will not get hurt too badly. That need for security is defensive. It is saying that you are not confident in your decision, but hope it works. Hope is an ineffective way to make any decision. Hope is not knowing. Knowing has a much higher probability of success. Knowing requires overcoming our basic fear. It requires the least amount of rationalization and defensiveness of which you are capable. Knowing requires the confidence of overcoming our fear of showing and asserting ourselves and change and success.

A better way to own a stock is to buy a stock with an effective leader. Regrettably, there have been few flexible, aggressive leaders. Sam Walton (Wal-Mart) and Jack Welch (GE) are two of the exceptions. Both had largely overcome their fear. They were aggressive and successful. Defensively we are afraid of even the word aggressive. We put negative connotations to it. Conversely, we want our athletic teams, our companies and our armies to be aggressive. That implies we think aggressiveness wins. However, since World War II, our country has chosen to avoid showing and asserting our power. We hide our potency even from ourselves. We rationalize that aggressiveness is not nice. Nice implies it will get us acceptance and love. We are afraid to speak up or give a speech before a crowd. It frightens us because it is showing and asserting ourselves even though the audience is for us. However, showing and asserting and success get acceptance and love. If you show something, there is something there to admire and love. Otherwise, we are neuter/protoplasm. Leaders show themselves. Why not own a stock with a leader, if you truly want to succeed. Many people want to be in the market, even if they are losing. They prefer to have a bad deal rather than no deal, including marriage. Their need for attachment is a testimonial to their fear of aloneness, separation and independence – self.

Fear is pervasive in all endeavors. For example, it is apparent on Sunday afternoons among professional tour golfers. The last nine holes of the tournament are when anxiety and fear takes control. These best golfers in the world often defeat themselves. Their fear of showing and asserting themselves and change and success takes over. Like all fields, golf has had few leaders in its history. The same goes for our official leaders in government domestic or foreign. Because of our own need for security we elevate politicians, bosses, professional people and fathers to power, wisdom and authority. We elevate them to try to assuage our need for security. We long for a powerful or surrogate father. We reduce, withdraw and negate ourselves in order to prevent showing and asserting ourselves. Our need for security dominates. We recruit financial advisors to invest our money, hoping they will carry us to victory. Financial advisors make a living investing other peoples money. If a financial advisor could successfully pick stocks for himself, why would he tolerate with having to put up with investors? Financial advisors are like other people. They are afraid to put themselves on the line. They are dominated by their fear and need for security as well. Our quest for money is a quest for security. Stocks are even called securities. We want security. We want protection. We want to be carried as we were in infancy and childhood.

We want more money and love no matter how much we already have. Love and money are security. We don't feel we can have too much security. Because of our fear, we are more insecure than we have the openness and courage to recognize. In part, that accounts for the repetitiveness in this text. Our dominating fear is the reason we rationalize and attempt to hide ourselves. We are block out artists; otherwise this insight would have been understood long ago. Oddly, on a deeper subconscious level we have understood our fear. Our conscious and mostly unconscious understanding into ourselves is why we have been able to continue to avoid this fear and understanding with rationalized, defensive security decisions. We compromise and defeat ourselves. We are escape artists from self. Our business schools are good at teaching the mechanics of business. However, there is little understanding or effort to teach independent, flexible, aggressive, effective, successful thinking and functioning. To do so would require the institution understood its own fear and had overcome its emotional dominance. Understanding as to why we make decisions and our fear dominance should be the most necessary aspects of education from an early age. It can open us and somewhat reduce our fear.

Business and education's obligation should be to succeed first, not the protection of the management and teachers. Using the company for their own self protection compromises or destroys the company, the management and the shareowners. If we limit our business to the only business in which we are involved, we are stifling ourselves. We are victims of our fear of flexibility, change and success. Business is not limited to one product or one industry. Business is open and unlimited. The only limit is self-imposed by management's fear and inhibition. The CEO's first focus is often on pleasing investors, Wall Street and the next quarter's earnings report. That distracts and inhibits his flexibility and independence – his freedom. He abdicates self. He is encouraging the people who want him to carry them to victory to run his business. The CEO's fear and need for security determines his degree of success or its avoidance. Many want the security of golden parachutes instead of driving the company to success and thence the stock price. The development and use of the corporation is largely to act as a protective father.

Sam Walton, founder of Wal-Mart was an unusual, independent person including being a father image to his employees. He had largely overcome his fear of showing and asserting himself and of change and success. Sam Walton had courage. He often visited his stores and associates. He listened to them. He showed interest in them. That gave his associates more security, confidence and desire to show interest in their company, customers and themselves. Showing personal interest – love - in your employees is an effective way to increase morale and reduce turnover. It ties the employees to the company. Walton believed strongly in the efficacy of aggressiveness. His ability to show and assert his interest and love elevated his employees and business. Every business is selling two commodities – their product and love. Every customer wants the security of both. Sam Walton delivered product and love at a low cost – security.

Employees want the security of the interest and love of the CEO – the surrogate father. After all, the CEO is the parent of the company and employees. Most CEO's know this unconsciously or even consciously, but are self stifled by their fear of showing and asserting their love. We are better mechanics than we are lovers. Our fear is our major obstacle, even in business.

Our country's CEO is the President. The President and Congress run the country's business. Of course, those people are just people, no matter how much we try to fantasize and elevate them. We try to elevate them to satisfy our own need for the security of a strong leader or father. Since politicians have their own fear, their need is for security. Being elected implies they are loved. Love is security.

Many laws are written to discriminate against equality and success. Our tax code is a major example. It is one of graduated taxes. The more a person earns the higher the tax rate percentage graduates. That is categorizing people. It is saying some people are less important than others are. I assume we have the laws because politicians believe there are more votes for a graduating discriminating tax than there is for equality. The politicians are dominated by their need for security to their own and our country's detriment. We stifle and punish aggressiveness, creativity and success. If a person commits the emotional crime of success, we penalize them with a higher tax fine. Yet we want our people, companies and our country to be number one. Paradoxically, we want them to succeed, but we want to punish them. This is further insight into our confusion created by our fear.

Having less flexibility and power includes having less money. We want more money no matter how much we already have. We often avoid saving. We arrange to have no reserve. We compromise our flexibility, independence and freedom. Having a reserve of money, ideas, rest, flexibility, conditioning/ strength, aggressiveness and love is potency. It is health. It is the basis of success. Governments don't do it. A few companies do. Those companies would be good candidates for ownership. Having savings and reserves implies they are disciplined and prefer the flexibility to take advantage of opportunities that surely occur. Many know this, but few can practice it. Having no savings usually implies the management is overreaching, quantity oriented and not running the business with reserve power. Those companies are more vulnerable to failure or take over by those with reserve strength. Those companies are good short sales possibilities. Conrad Hilton bought failing hotels after someone else built them. However, he bought them at a discount. He had reserve strength. To make effective decisions we have to overcome our security need; that is our fear of showing and asserting ourselves, change and success. The hardest decision in life is the one that attempts to overcome our fear. After attempting to define the basis of success in business and life, I can make a suggestion with only mild humor. Since Sam Walton had reduced fear and was such a success in business, I assume he could have been a success for our country as president. The major advances in society have come from individuals, not the insecurity of committees.

III. Relations

Our fear is dominant is relations. We mostly choose relations that hopefully accept us. Our relations are usually an attempt to gain security. Being loved is the major basis of our need for security. Security is the primary purpose for marriage. Marriage is an effort to gain the security of love, as well as repeat the childhood security of family. Being loved implies you are protected. If love wanes, security wanes. If security wanes, interest wanes and the search for new security begins including divorce. Somewhat regrettable, both parties have married to get security. Often what we assume and hope to be love is actually need for security on the part of both. We say we love someone when we really mean we need someone for our own security. Love is giving; need is getting. Love requires we open, show and assert ourselves. To love is most frightening. Every person wants to be loved, but the major question is who can show and assert his/her love. Showing and asserting our love is possibly our most difficult undertaking. It exposes us. We avoid and hide our love, when that is what every person needs and wants from us, including ourselves from ourselves. Often we stage love, instead of feeling love. That is dishonest. It seldom works. The persons in which we are involved are usually more perceptive about us than we are about ourselves. Our lack of openness and our defensiveness are acts against ourselves. Our fear dominates.

Understanding our need for security allows a marriage the advantage of truth and openness. If we start with the correct premise we have a better chance of solving a problem. If we have the courage to understand our fear and need for security, we will probably have the courage to be objective and realistic about other understandings and decisions. Regrettably, we prefer to attribute our problems and dissatisfaction to surface, more tangible and safe reasons, including others, rather than the emotional and deeper reason. The problem is our fear and insecurity in our inability to attack self and our fear. Our fear of showing and asserting our love is the primary reason for the breakup of the marriage. The breakup of the marriage is the breakup of the family. The feeling of separation compounds the loss of the security of the family. We are alone and unprotected. This applies to all members of the family, including the one or ones that wanted the divorce. That loss of security accentuates our need for security. The results following the divorce are usually compromises and poor decisions in a somewhat desperate grab for security. The fear and grab for security often includes another ill-fated marriage because our dominating basic fears have not changed. Our desperation for security compromises our lives and often defeats us.

The breakup of the marriage is at least as hard on the children as on the divorced spouses. The children have lost what security or assumed security they had. The results are usually further withdrawal from showing and asserting themselves and change and success. They have had their security and therefore courage further reduced. Their fear is increased. They seldom have anyone available to support them, since their parents usually are in disarray themselves. The insecurity and fear of the whole family's ability to function is increased.

Love and money are our two basic securities. In a divorce love is dissipated and money usually is as well. When the money is not available, insecurity is increased even further. The primary reason for divorce is both parties' inability to show and assert their interest and love. The security of being loved is a major requisite to the ability to make and retain money. When there is money, if love dissipates, the money will often follow. Love and its security have the power to create, assert and succeed, including money.

Parent's fear of showing and asserting love is the primary reason for children not to acquire the ability to show and assert themselves, change, succeed or grow emotionally. The child lacks the security and encouragement and therefore the courage to grow, change, improve and succeed – to value and love self. We create clones, consciously and unconsciously, because of our fear and lack of understanding of our own fear. We rationalize their being like us to heredity or blood rather than accept our own emotional fear and its branding. We avoid self. Our purpose in parenting should be to create an independent, separate, informed, secure and successful individual of courage that can love and function effectively. If we were truly interested in our children for their individualism and their success, that would be a tribute to the parents. Regrettably, we often have children, so that the parent will have someone to love them, preferable permanently. The parent prefers the seeming security of unconditional love from the child. The parent wants security. That is not an effective premise to have children. The best parent or lover is the one that can show and assert their love from the boardroom to the bedroom. Passive is not exciting or stimulating. It is interest killing for the recipient, be it spouse, child, friend, acquaintance, employee, employer or co-worker. It communicates no interest or love by the inhibited instigator. The unusual person that doesn't have to be asked but volunteers and asserts interest and love is a confident and more effective person and parent. Speaking up is critical. Those people show something. They show self.

If a parent asks the child's opinion, it shows interest and respect for the child to think and vocalize it. It lets the child think they are respected, individual, valued and therefore loved. It underscores self. It allows the child to open and show and assert self. It reduces their basic fear. Parents that show little interest or love offer scant security to the child. This accentuates the child's fear of relations and his ability to show and assert his love. His self-stifling and withdrawal is increased. A secure, loving parent can create a secure, loving child.

In my opinion, the basis and cause of homosexuality is the pronounced fear of showing and asserting our love, especially to the opposite sex. Those persons are even more fearful than so-called non-homosexuals in closeness and love relationships. Showing and asserting their love is too frightening. They are hiding their sexuality.

Homosexuality has nothing to do with biology. Homosexuality is a product of our fear and enhanced need for security.

Regrettably, our need for love and its security follows us for life, unless understood, absorbed and reduced. I doubt it can be completely overcome. We spend a lifetime searching for love and security. From early childhood we elevate father and symbolic fathers beyond their capacity in order to attempt to placate our fear and need for security. We want a strong protective and loving father that can beat up the guy down the street. We have the same desire and need in our company leader or the president of our country. Our fear and insecurity from childhood of what might happen to us is pervasive and consuming.

One of the most profound paradoxes of love is closeness. We want to be loved and close to the one we want to love us. Paradoxically, the closer we get to that person the more frightened we become and we withdraw. Our fear of showing and asserting our love dominates. However, we want someone to love us. That is not democratic or equitable. We want the security of getting, but cannot give. This pattern originates in infancy and early childhood. In infancy we had the unconditional love and security of mother. She was our world. We were the center of her world with her full attention and nurturing, love and its security. We controlled love. We were the king of our domain. Beginning with the terrible twos, we began to realize we were losing total dominance over our love and security, which was mother. That was the beginning of love lost. It was the beginning of our turning away from mother to our hoped for surrogate security - father. It undermined our trust and therefore our commitment to love and closeness. That was the beginning of our lifelong fear and it's by-product anger. Not being in control or getting what we want creates anger. Our world began to become competitive. Our fear began to generate our anger as our security began to disintegrate. We felt rejected. We lost our most valued possession, our security. That was the beginning of our fear of closeness. We became fearful that with closeness became separation and loss of security. That is much too painful. It is a graphic and overwhelming imprint of the threat of closeness and its cost. Trust is slow to build, but quick and easy to dissipate. Until recognized and reduced, trust remains a dominating lifelong force in our fear of loving. However, the joy and fulfillment of love/ security becomes a lifelong search to duplicate the unconditional love and security of infancy. The more a person needs to control another person as in infancy with mother, the more insecure that person is. This basic need and drive is insight into the significance of infancy and emotion. Emotion and feelings are our first impression. We have feelings before we can think. Intellect develops later. We respond to our feelings. Our loss of love accentuates our fear of showing and asserting our feelings of love. We are too afraid we will lose it again. That is too painful. Our need for security is the basis of our fear and therefore our functioning. The loss of love and security is our dominating fear. Therefore our decisions and functionings are arranged to avoid showing and asserting ourselves – our love. If we don't show anything supposedly we have nothing to lose and therefore will not be hurt. Our fear of showing and asserting our love is the reason all families are dysfunctional in varying degrees. Our fear is a successful upside down pyramid. Unless we overcome our fear, we just exist. I prefer we live.

Our effort and rationalization is to blame our dilemma on others or circumstances. That avoids the truth and responsibility. The problem is self. If we take self out of the equation, we avoid solving the problem and its success. We want to understand why our automobile is not working properly. When we recognize the problem, we fix the car. We want it to be dependable and run effectively – succeed. However, when it comes to ourselves and our fears, we rationalize and avoid the truth. Do we think more of our car than ourselves; or is self and our fear just too frightening to even contemplate? Every person has this same problem. Living is difficult. It is hardball, but we try to play it as butterfly netting. We want strength, power, freedom, acceptance, money, love and success. Most unfortunately because of our fear of showing and asserting ourselves, we avoid going after it. We avoid our potentially effective firepower and success. We are tentative and indecisive. We are not sure whether we want security or success. We respond instead of assert, initiate and create. That withdrawal to hoped for security compounds our insecurity. Our attempted self-protection from our fear diminishes living and life. Our fear grows from this somewhat hidden root, the same as the root of a tree obscures its power and expansiveness.

IV.
Fear: The Primary Cause of Disease – Heart

Fear is our primary and worst disease. Numerous other diseases are by-products of our fear. Understanding the cause of our fear is necessary to begin to overcome several major diseases. We have heretofore focused on a biologic approach that has and will continue to leave us wanting. By avoiding emotion and our fear, we have perpetuated our illness and dying. Until we recognize our dominating fear, we will continue to compromise and defeat ourselves, including health. The purpose of this phase of this understanding is to specifically define the primary cause of disease, regardless of how it threatens our previous avoidance, concepts, defenses, prejudices and rationalizations – our fears. The truth is more important and much longer lasting than all of us.

Fear is the primary cause of heart disease. As has been repeatedly stated, our basic fear of showing and asserting ourselves and change and success is also the primary cause of heart disease. We have not consciously recognized our fear. Because of the depth, magnitude, anxiety and seeming threat of our fear, we have chosen to remain unconscious. Therefore, we demonstrate our fear by our functioning, rationalizations, defensiveness and avoidance, including the shock of heart attacks. For one example, the majority of heart attacks occur on Monday mornings. That is when people have to go back to work and show and assert themselves. For some that is too frightening. In essence, we lock up with fear. That heart attack is the by-product of our emotional fear. The degree of our fear is the basis of the frequency and degree of the self imposed attack. We are so dominated by our fear of showing and asserting ourselves and change and success that we block out and avoid our feelings and our fear. We bottle up our feelings until we erupt. We do not vent our feelings. Venting is showing and asserting ourselves. Venting is healthy. When we are emotionally closed, that resonates throughout our system.

When we are frightened and stressed, we are not relaxed and our cardiovascular system reflects it. It is uptight, convoluted and somewhat brittle. It is tentative, not decisive or smooth flowing. It is a product of our fear at that time. It is not content. It is not relaxed; it is insecure. We are what we feel and believe on a deeper, mostly unconscious level. The primary cause of heart attack is our basic fear of showing and asserting ourselves. Our enemy is self, because of our fear.

People, especially men, think in order to be manly, we have to be strong for our mate, children, others and ourselves. We have to appear powerful. Anything less would appear sissy, weak or cowardly. As with many things involving our feelings, the opposite is true. By attempting to appear strong we are denying our feelings. By not being relaxed and flexible we are bottling ourselves up and building pressure. We are dishonest in order to hide our feelings. We are denying self. We are inhibiting and stifling self. This self-stifling puts added pressure on our circulatory system. When we pump up enough pressure, the system can blow out, including the heart.

Now that the percentage of women working is increasing, we are seeing a higher incidence of heart disease among them. In past times, societies made it acceptable and even a requirement for women to be passive and subservient to man. It made it necessary to avoid showing and asserting themselves in order to be accepted. In part, this was appealing to women, since they didn't have to deal with their fear of showing and asserting themselves. This was and is also appealing to men, since women as dependent persons were no threat to man. Men had control over their chattel. Control implies no threat. The more fearful a person, the more need of that person for control.

As society begins to open somewhat, women begin to show and assert themselves and change and succeed. The women's liberation movement was a turning point in society. Women begin to invade the business, professional and political domain of the former world of men. That was wonderful for women, but frightening. The freedom of choice was independence and success. It was exciting and satisfying, but also anxiety provoking. It is a double bladed sword. The joy was freedom. However the fear was freedom. Therefore, with the increase in showing and asserting ourselves, change and success comes increased fear and heart attacks. That will continue until we recognize this cause and begin to absorb and incorporate these basics.

We are seeing an increased incidence of heart problems in young people. The parents fear of showing and asserting themselves and of change and success is the primary reason. Without the courage to love, the parent cannot offer security to the child. The child is a jewel that needs love and thoughtful polishing. If the child is not raised with the security of interested and loving parents the risk of heart attacks and other diseases increases – success is avoided.

More recently the breakup of the family is accentuating the problems of the heart. The family is the basis of what security the child has. With the breakup of the family the child's security is further undermined. Because of already being often accused of their faults, plus their own doubts and accusations, they feel somewhat responsible for the breakup of the marriage and family home - their security. Their thoughts include what they might have done caused and added to the breakup. In other words, they should have not been so assertive. They should be more passive and self-stifled. That thought further compounds their fear of showing and asserting themselves. Their confidence is further diminished. They lock up and withdraw even more. That self-stifling lock up increases the possibility of heart attacks.

Heart disease is our number one killer. With the breakup of the family, I assume it will remain so. With this insight, we can begin to solve the major part of our heart problem. While that is wonderful and important, there are other benefits. The financial gain from avoiding heart disease to individuals, families, business and government is incalculable. The health costs to government for

Medicare, Medicaid, and research is an overwhelming financial burden. This understanding can begin to change that pattern. Perpetuating our fear will assure the rising cost of health. The loss of productivity is a major financial burden to society. Improving health and productivity improves the bottom line of business and government. Improving the bottom line enhances the security of the management.

V. Depression

Fear is the basis of depression. Depression is the number one disease worldwide. The degree of depression ranges from occasional to full time. It includes every person in varying degrees. It is an emotional disease. It is another by-product of our fear. Other diseases are often mistaken for what actually is depression. We prefer to have a tangible or biological disease rather than one that is related to emotion, feelings and mental. The avoidance of this basic cause negates the probability of overcoming the problem. We have again started with the wrong premise. This avoidance of our emotions and our fear is an insight into our fear of our emotions and feelings. We prefer a rational, defensive and safe answer that excludes self, rather than the truth. Defensiveness and success are not compatible. The question then becomes why do we avoid self – the source of our power, strength and success.

Our fear is of the involvement and participation of

self. Depression is avoidance. It is self-suppression. It is our hiding. It is withdrawal, even to the fetal position in the extreme cases of fear. Our withdrawal is an attempt to not be involved. To be involved, we have to show and assert ourselves. We have to show up, stand up and participate. That is too frightening for some people. We are all intellectually smart, but restrain, rationalize and withdraw ourselves. Our emotional fear overwhelms our intellectual smart. We choose to use our thinking to try to rationalize our avoidance of showing and asserting ourselves. We withdraw into depression and avoid the seeming risk of living.

Our fear of opening and showing ourselves and change and success is the primary cause of depression. The alternative to showing and asserting ourselves is our self-imposed depression. We withdraw and depress ourselves defensively in order to not show ourselves. That fear dictates we depress ourselves. This attempted self-protection and escape compounds and perpetuates our fear and its depression requirement. Depression is an act against ourselves. Depression is a form of non-living. It is existing only. It is a form of death and feels like dying.

The majority of people in the world have a milder degree of depression. When we are not speaking up, we are in depression. Not speaking up in the family to spouse or children is self-imposed stifling depression. It is a significant cause of poor relations or divorce in the family. Conversely, continual talking or a happy façade is not honest. It is self-stifling of a real feeling of fear and anger that every person has. The happy façade is a rationalization. This self-imposed depression can create other diseases. We prefer to label depression only when is it in its extreme occurrence. However, we all know, we are hiding and depressing our fear and feelings in numerous ways. We are afraid to open. We are escape artists from self.

VI. Certain Cancers

Certain cancers are directly or indirectly by-products of our fear. In part, cancer seems to be a disease related to aging. As we get older our system becomes less resilient. It is not a growing, expanding aggressive system. It becomes a weakened system. It becomes a more complacent, passive and even defensive system. That sounds like our personality and its fear dominance. It is. Different components breakdown. The components that we abuse the most seem more vulnerable to attack by cancer. Some of that abuse would be from smoking. alcohol, drugs, exposure to sunlight, asbestos and other foreign objects. I think quantity and quality of foods could be included. Nearly all of these irritants are self-induced. In recent years we have become more aware of what these irritants are. Regrettably, we know of these obstacles to better health, but many people choose to continue to subject themselves to these enemies of health. We say we want to avoid cancer but continue smoking, taking drugs, abusing alcohol and exposing ourselves to sunlight among others. Why do we do that? They are all somewhat desperate grabs for security. Our emotional need for security overwhelms our intellectual understanding. Drugs and alcohol are attempted escapes from our feelings, anxiety and pain – our fear of showing and asserting ourselves. These escape attempts weaken our system plus our emotional courage to fight. We avoid our aggressiveness and potency. Our fear helps create the potential real problem of cancer. We compromise and defeat ourselves and then want the medical profession to save us. Can we help ourselves even with this understanding?

Does our fear invite attack by aggressive cancer cells? Cancer may attack the weakest adversary or the weakest component of even a stronger adversary. The strongest often attack the weakest in animal, nature and countries. If we all have cancer cells within us, why doesn't everyone have cancer? Of course, the more insecure people weaken themselves with security rationalizations such as smoking, drugs, alcohol, food, lack of exercise, etc. Those more insecure fearful people are inviting attack by cancer and other diseases. I believe the major antidote to cancer is understanding and reducing our fear and its need for security. Besides that obvious avoidance, there may be other factors. Cancer cells are usually conceded to be aggressive. If we are afraid of our own aggressiveness are we aiding the aggressive cancer cells in their march over us? Does cancer, like people, animals and armies avoid attacking strength? If so, it is necessary that people overcome their fear of their aggressiveness and success. If cancer does unleash its attack, it is critical to out aggressive the aggressive cancer. When you believe you are going to show yourself, be aggressive and succeed, you are more confident. If you are more confident, you are more reliable. If you are more relaxed your system and cells operate more smoothly and efficiently. You are not fearful. You have understood and largely overcome your fear of your own aggressiveness. You are powerful. You are offensive, not defensive. You know you will succeed not just hope, wish or think you will. Hope is believing you are going to fail. Hope implies you have little or no control over the situation. Knowing is not being afraid of your aggressiveness or success. If we are not changing, expanding and improving, we are declining. We are stagnating and vegetating. We are just protoplasm. We are existing, not living. That makes us vulnerable to attack. In cancer we have to fight aggressively to conquer the intruder into our domain, our fortress, our well-armed and powerful empire.

Smoking is major cause of cancer and heart disease. The accepted consensus is that smoking is a chemical addiction. I disagree with that surface, seemingly obvious, but defensive conclusion. If smoking is a chemical addition, then why aren't second hand smokers addicted? Some smokers will tell you smoking is a nasty habit. Some tell you they don't like the smoke or smell. Smokers are well aware of the dangers of smoking. They find the constant reminders repetitive and boring. You could say it makes them feel so rejected, unloved and nervous that they decide to have another smoke. If smokers find so many faults with smoking then why smoke? As usual, emotion and fear dominates their mostly unconscious decision making and therefore functioning. Smokers get a certain satisfaction and calmness from smoking. In times of increased stress, smoking is somewhat reassuring. Since need for security is the basis of our functioning, smoking is a desperate grab for security. The security of smoking is sucking. It is an attempted repeat of the security of mother in our infancy, our initial imprint, impression and greatest security. That need for mother's security overwhelms all the negative and frightening threats of cancer and heart disease. We choose the possibility or probability of sickness and death over our lifelong search for security at any cost. If we could overcome that need for the seeming security of smoking, we could reduce cancers from the mouth to the stomach, including lung cancer. It would also reduce the degree of heart disease. Smoking's grab for security is a misdirected act against ourselves.

VII. Asthma

Asthma is a disease that makes if difficult to breathe deeply and freely. It can start in early childhood or later. It is a shortage of breath. If can be quite frightening and even cause death. What is the cause of asthma? Several environmental intrusions precipitate asthma. Weather, pollen, dust, chemicals and smoke are some of the environmental causes of asthma. They are outside invaders. A reasonable question would be why some people succumb to these agitators and others do not. Does it have anything to do with sensitivity? Is the sensitivity to the outside influences or to our emotional vulnerability?

Our fear is a major cause of asthma. When our security is threatened we tighten up. Our fear takes our breath away. We label it asthma. Our fear is inhibiting and stifling. As we become more frightened and uptight our system and passages become constricted. As our passages tightened and shrink, breathing is reduced and labored.

That compounds our fear and further tightens our breathing passages. We are not relaxed. We do not have a relaxed, smooth, effectively functioning system. We are stifled. We call it asthma. We put a medical label on it, instead of calling it a manifestation of our fear. As we continue to see, we are fearful of showing and asserting ourselves. If we are afraid of showing and asserting ourselves, we are self-stifled. Asthma is fear of showing and asserting ourselves. Overcoming our fear reduces asthma. Overcoming our fear enhances our freedom-from asthma.

VIII. Alzheimer's

Alzheimer's disease is considered a severe neurological disorder marked by progressive dementia as irreversible deterioration of intellectual faculties with accompanying emotional disturbance resulting from organic brain disorder. Alzheimer's is a disease of seeming involuntary and progressive loss of memory. It seems that is the generally accepted belief. I disagree. Alzheimer's is an emotional disease, not a biological one. It is a disease that starts early in childhood and progresses almost imperceptibly throughout life. It culminates to the degree in which it finally is officially medically defined as Alzheimer's disease. I suggest that Alzheimer's may change the brain, not the other way around. Why should the brain be different from muscles or other organs? It we don't nourish and exercise, that is, challenge and use it, does it become atrophied, as does the rest of our body? I believe so. The brain chemistry follows the lead of our emotional fear. Emotional courage improves the brain chemistry. We all know of people that operate effectively with ninety-year-old brains. Alzheimer's is the mostly unconsciously planned withdrawal from participation in functioning life. It is withdrawal to dependence and being taken care of. It is avoidance of functioning on your own. What is the purpose of this subtle and almost invisible but seemingly irreversible or unconscious decision? The purpose for this withdrawal to Alzheimer's is our need for security. Our need for security dominates our functioning in varying degrees. The degree of need for security is higher in those people that retreat to Alzheimer's. Alzheimer's is by-product of our fear of coping and showing and asserting ourselves. Alzheimer's is attempted reversion to the unconscious, but well implanted security of mother in infancy. The imprint of the seeming security of infancy and mothers' love and protection has reasserted itself. We then avoid the stress and fear of making decisions or showing and asserting ourselves. Our fear and need for security dominates – including Alzheimer's.

IX. Parkinson's

Parkinson's disease is defined as a progressive nervous disease of later life, characterized by muscular tremor, slowing of movement, partial facial paralysis, peculiarity of gait and posture and weakness. It is generally believed to be of biological origin, however, the specific cause has not been identified. The search for a biological answer continues. I suggest it is a product of our basic emotional fear, as are other major diseases. Most or all of the characteristics of Parkinson's imply a relation to anxiety. In my opinion the anxiety and resulting characteristics are products of our basic fear. As in Alzheimer's and other diseases, the seeds of Parkinson's are planted in infancy and early childhood. The tremors, slowing of movements, partial facial paralysis, peculiar gait, stooped posture and weakness are by-products of our fear. Our fear of opening and showing and asserting ourselves and change and success are the primary causes of Parkinson's disease. Parkinson's, like Alzheimer's is gradual withdrawal from participation in life. It is a product of our mostly unconscious desire to be taken care of. When our fear becomes intolerable we lock up and Parkinson's starts to engulf us. Our slowing down and slowness is a stage of withdrawal. We become bent, crumbling and feel defeated and exhausted. We increasingly avoid showing and asserting ourselves. We become a façade, even more so than normal people do. Our lockup includes our whole system, often including our bowel movement. We literally and figuratively can't get the excrement out. When our fear locks us up, it is debilitating and demeaning. The cause of Parkinson's is fear of loss of security. Increasing security can reduce Parkinson's and possibly even the more severe Alzheimer's. The security of love and the provider of interest and love are the key to unlocking Parkinson's. That interest can slowly get the victim to open. To get the victim to start talking is the beginning of reducing Parkinson. Talking is venting and relieving the pressure and stress of our anger/fear. Talking is therapeutic. Talking is showing and asserting yourself. Parkinson's is a by-product of lack of security – our fear.

X. Immune System

Our immune system is a major component of health. We want our immune system to protect us from the onslaught of illness. We somewhat fantasize that our immune system is a separate entity from ourselves. It is not. Our immune system is a by-product of our fear or courage. If we are fearful and passive our immune system is likewise. If we are aggressive and up front, so is our immune system. We want our immune system to be aggressive and succeed, but are afraid of our own aggressiveness. Paradoxically, we admire the student that is working two jobs to get through college. That student is aggressive. Stifling our aggressiveness/anger is dishonest. Stifling and/or denying our aggressive anger inhibits the natural activity of our functioning including our immune systems. As we bottle up our system, it becomes stagnant. If a river slows or stops its flow, it becomes vulnerable to disease. It can't cleanse itself. It becomes easy prey for various attackers and diseases. It is not flowing, vibrant, strong and alive. Insects attack weakened trees and crops. Likewise, our lack of aggressiveness, our weakness and fear invites attack.

XI. Obesity and Anorexia Nervosa

Obesity is defined as extreme fat. By some standards obesity is reaching epidemic status. Anorexia nervosa is sometimes defined as a pathological condition occurring mostly in young women that is marked by aversion to food.

Health professionals have been publicizing the dangers of being overweight for years. Recommendations have included diets of all sorts and exercise. Most obese people are familiar with this advice. Even then can they change and succeed? Unfortunately, these approaches have only limited and temporary effects, at best. However, we continue to eat until we overload the boat. We sink ourselves. Obesity and anorexia have the same basic origin. They are by-products of our fear and need for security. Being overweight is a result of overeating or drinking. Overeating is our need to get love. Drinking alcohol is a need to reduce our anxiety and to escape our fear. They both are misdirected grabs for security. Those security grabs are acts against ourselves. Both are mouth, sucking and taste gratification. Mouth was an original taste of security and mother's love. Our addiction is our need for the security of love.

Anorexia nervosa produces underweight to even frail people. They have an aversion to food and eating. Their purpose is to be even thinner, though they are already thin. Their longing for their rationalized thinness is that they will finally be accepted and loved. They believe then that they will finally get the security of love. Their misplaced obsession often creates just the opposite. They are often not loved, sometimes even scorned. Their fear of showing and asserting themselves has reduced them to almost showing nothing, including physical. Their premise to get love and security was erroneous. Their thinness was an act against themselves. As long as we do not understand that our basic fear is the cause of our illness and attack it, we will remain insatiable in our quest for love and security. These are the more obvious diseases of our fear.

XII. Summary

The intention of this understanding is to define the basis of our mostly unconscious decision making and therefore our functioning in work, health and relations – our lives. If we don't understand why, that is, the cause of problems, solving any problem becomes an exercise in luck or probably impossible. There is a reason for everything. Understanding the basis of why we make decisions is the basis of all our functioning. To understand why we function, we have to open-up. If we are not open, we can't tolerate different or frightening ideas. We can't change. If we are closed, we are self stifled and locked up. We resort to a life of rationalization and defensiveness-fear.

As this insight has attempted to explain, emotion is more influential than intellect in our functioning. This is contrary to what we have been taught. We have preferred to believe our intellect is our salvation. We focus on our thinking because we are afraid of our feelings/emotion. Thinking and defensive rationalization is seemingly safe compared to our feelings. Our feelings include our fear, anger, hurt, joy and our love. Showing and asserting those feelings is too frightening. Why are our feelings so dominate? We become aware of our feelings in infancy, long before our intellect. We can feel our feelings, but not our intellect. That initial imprint is profound and lifelong. In infancy we are totally dependent. That dependence focuses on mother. She becomes our lifeline. She fills our basic and primary need. She is our security. That need for security is a product of our feelings. She overcomes our helplessness. She provides touching, coddling, smiling, soothing words, singing, sustenance and love. She likes us. She fulfills our need for security. We like those things and begin to show it with our response, smiling and joy. We need an attentive, loving mother to protect us. If interest and love is not provided, we show that with our displeasure. We rebel and begin to withdraw, usually for life. We respond to a feeling of love or rejection. Feelings dominate from infancy throughout life. We get our feelings hurt more easily than we get our intellect hurt. Our need for security is our paramount need. Our dominating fear in life is of loss of security. That fear is the basis and compromise of our most unconscious decision making and therefore our functioning. We have control of our largely unconditional love of our mother. We would prefer to retain that control of largely unconditioned love from mother. We prefer to retain that control of our security since it was the height of our secure feelings. Life after infancy was devoted to attempting to regain that security utopia. Did that make infancy the central point and security capitol of our lives? It would seem so, since under extreme stress we often return to the fetal position.

Our intellect begins to develop after infancy. The terrible twos are the beginning of the intellectual recognition that we are losing our control and security. This loss of our security is the beginning of our fear. The loss of our security is the beginning of our anger. Since we soon learn that our anger can get us in trouble or rejection, we start early to attempt to stifle and hide our anger. We try to appear nice. We are fearful we might otherwise get our feelings hurt. It is so frightening that we spend a lifetime trying to hide our anger and fear even from ourselves. We focus more on our intellect. Our ability to think becomes advanced in relation to those things outside ourselves. We can figure out how to go the moon and other technological marvels. Our imagination is unlimited when it comes to intellectual activities. However, when it comes to personal emotional understandings we have continued to avoid, inhibit and block our feelings. We avoid opening and showing and asserting ourselves and change and success. Those fears are the basis of our security. They are the opposite of being taken care of. They are the basis of taking care of success and ourselves. We are afraid to even consider we are all insecure. We don't open self to self. We avoid independence, our potency and freedom.

One of the most brilliant intellectuals in history was Albert Einstein. We are still learning to understand things he advocated decades ago. Einstein was the intellectual genius. However, when it came to emotions, Einstein was quite normal. He had difficulty with female and male relationships. He could not control relationships to his satisfaction or security need. When it came to closeness and love, Einstein was more fearful than successful. His need was to get love. He was afraid to show and assert his love. His life was spent in part searching for the security of mother's love.

We are asking how some individuals could need the security of their mothers, even when they had bad, not caring or non-loving mothers. Since the infant is so dependent, even a bad mother is better than no mother. Mother is the child's lifeline. In instances where there is little or no touching or caring, only food, the child can wither and even die. The more inhibited, fearful and less caring a mother, the higher degree of fear and resultant anger in the child.

Our most consuming emotional feeling is when we are loved. It is the quickest and easiest way we are brought to tears. It is our consuming security. Of course, it requires someone that can love. When we are loved our security and therefore our courage to show and assert ourselves is increased. When we are loved, we feel acceptable. We feel it somewhat less frightening to show and assert ourselves. Our attitudes become more positive. Our withdrawal and hiding is diminished. We even become proud of self. We have the courage to show and assert our love. We have the courage and power to succeed.

Our fear is pervasive in all our functioning, including health. Several diseases have been defined earlier in this text. In all diseases our fear creates a defeatist attitude. That attitude increases our vulnerability and invitation to disease. One example is cancer. When we overcome cancer we say we are survivors. That is a defeatist and passive attitude. I think people that overcome cancer are victors. The cancer was defeated. This is insight into our fear of our own aggressiveness and success. Our aggressiveness is so frightening that we arrange to not even be aware of what we are doing to ourselves. We are victors over cancer, so why not recognize and express it. We succeed. Cancer is defeated. We imply we should be humble.

However, if we succeed at anything but deny it by being humble we are dishonest. We have denied success. Being humble is fear of showing and asserting ourselves. Henry David Thoreau put it thusly: "The mass of men lead lives of quiet desperation". I think this insight explains that fear.

Our fear is the major shortcoming in business. We have thousands of good managers, but only a handful of leaders. Managers respond to situations. Leaders create and are flexible. A leader is aggressive and independent. A manager needs the security of a committee. A leader can show and assert himself/herself. A leader can change and succeed. Managers lack that courage. A leader that can show and assert his/her love toward his or her employees enhances their security. They are confident to show and assert themselves with suggestions to improve the company. The absenteeism and turnover is reduced. The employees' security is increased. They are loved by their father or leader. There can be certain restraints on what a business can pay people. The only restraint on interest and love is the fear of the leader to show and assert his/her love.

A leader has the confidence to be decisive, but has the security to admit mistakes and make changes. His/her leadership increases productivity. A leader can put his/her company in any business and make it work and succeed. Communicating is a significant obstacle to society. Our fear of opening and asserting ourselves is the primary cause of our lack of communication. It inhibits talking, writing and loving. Communicating is giving. Lack of communicating is a need to gain security. Lack of communicating is stifling of self by self. Advertising could focus more on peoples' need for the security of love in my opinion. A major purpose of advertising would be a lasting imprint and meeting peoples need. Since love is our primary need, its imprint is deep and permanent. To weave love into advertising will be a fulfilling part of every potential customer's need.

Several major medical institutions have seen this understanding of our fear as the primary cause of heart disease. No one has attempted to refute any part of this insight. Regrettably, these medical institutions have chosen to avoid it, the Hippocratic oath notwithstanding. Of course, the security of the medical profession is our illness. Their business is repair. This insight is prevention – cause and why. The medical profession's avoidance of this understanding is insight into their ability to avoid and depress ourselves. Their fear of the loss of their security is depressing for them. If we have something to look forward to, depression is reduced and life can be enhanced and extended in my opinion. Depression is the self-imposed withdrawal from living or even life.

To be responsible requires we have the courage to admit a mistake. If we can't admit a mistake, we can't change, improve or succeed. Not admitting a mistake implies we are perfect. Rationalizing that we are perfect means we don't have to change. Thinking we are perfect means we are inflexible, even frozen. Thinking we are perfect is insight into our insecurity. Responsibility requires we reduce our fear. The more responsible a person, the more open, honest, assertive, flexible, loving, effective and successful that person is. You can trust a responsible person. A responsible person can trust themselves and their decisions. To love requires a responsible, secure person. We often mistake love for need; that is need for the security of love. Need for security is getting.

Showing and asserting your love is giving love. Giving love is giving security along with the good feeling it generates in the giver. To love is power. Getting over our fear of showing and asserting our love is probably our most difficult task. To be a responsible person requires the courage to choose the truth over our need for security. The more insecure a person, the less responsible that person is.

Our fear is of loss of our security. That is the basis of our functioning. Our sexuality is a major part of our security. We hide our sexuality behind our clothing. We show our eyes, ears, hands, etc. While we all have the same sexual parts, we act as if ours are sacred. We often even hide them from our spouse. However, our intrigue is with sex. That includes movies, television, magazines, books, etc. We are curious, but withdraw and live vicariously. We hear the expression that our brains are in our sexual apparatus. Yet, we hide our own sexuality because it is a major aspect of our security. Its loss becomes a dominating fear. If we show and assert ourselves we are afraid we will be criticized or rejected. We fear if we show and assert ourselves-stick it out-we will have our penis cutoff-our worst and dominating fear. The same applies for females. Our fear is loss of our sexuality-our security. This is why opening and reducing our defenses is most frightening and difficult. However, that is the requisite to changing, improving and succeeding-reducing our fear. You see little boys holding their penis for the reassurance that it is still there. When they are older, you see them check to see if their treasure is still there. When they are baseball players and have made a hit and are on first base, they often unconsciously check their sexual part for security. Our dominating fear is of loss of security, starting with our sexuality. Contrary to popular surface opinion, sexy is the understanding and courage to overcome our fear of showing and asserting our love in my opinion. Sexy is the power to give love. Our core need for security is a successful upside down pyramid.

Father becomes the focus of our security need. Our need for the security of father starts in childhood and remains until death. Father is elevated and fantasized to be our protector – our security. We prefer to believe father is strong and can beat up the daddy down the street. We prefer to believe our company or country's president is stronger than the competition. We think our doctor or other people that we are dependent upon are more capable than they actually are. We deceive ourselves in our search for security. Even our religions have God as a male and he is often referred to as father or our savior from our fear and insecurity. Regrettably, we still have religious wars. That has been going on for millenniums. While most religions preach peace, our need to control requires we fight wars. In part, we are pitting our God/ father against theirs. We are saying our God is better, stronger and more protective than yours is. A protective God/father is necessary to our consuming need for security. Devotion to your religion implies rejection of my religion. Rejection of my security is a fighting word. Our fear dominates.

Plato said, "The life which is unexamined is not worth living". This insight defines our basic fear of our emotions and self. It is looking in the mirror. This understanding is frightening. It is hardball, not just butterfly netting. With this basic understanding of our dominating fear, we have the basic premise to begin to reduce and even overcome our fear. As we reduce our fear, our flexibility, aggressiveness, success and courage is increased.

54

Being fearful is human and universal. It is nothing to be ashamed of. Understanding this cause of our debilitating fear and not attacking it is insight into the dominance of our fear. That is also an act against ourselves. Fortunately or unfortunately, depending on your viewpoint, we cannot make effective decisions unless we can overcome our fear of showing and asserting ourselves. Security decisions don't succeed. We avoid and procrastinate. Procrastination is fear of showing and asserting ourselves. In health, procrastination is an indicator of several future diseases. We can show and assert our love to our infants, but why not to our spouse? Overcoming our fear of showing and asserting our love liberates us from our emotional paralysis and prisons - our fear. It allows the efficacy, success, joy and loving of self – of living. Integrity requires courage.

We want to be powerful, effective and healthy, but hide our aggressiveness. For example: the United States has not completed or succeeded in war since World War II, even though it had the power and expertise, but not the emotional courage. We neuter ourselves. This text has consistently emphasized our fear of showing and asserting ourselves and change and success. Consequently, with no offense to anyone, there is a bottom line to our functioning in work, health and relations – life. If you can't stick it out, you can't stick it in. Fear is the basis of our functioning. Fortunately, if we start with the correct premise, we have the basis of getting the correct results. In functioning, the correct premise is self. If we avoid self with its fear our premise is rationalized, defensive and avoids the truth. Overcoming our fear means self has a significant advantage. We have the emotional courage and good fortune of showing and asserting ourselves and being able to change and be successful. We have the liberation, freedom, power and efficacy of - self. Self is our answer.